I Can Write
All
Through the Year

by

Kathy Dunlavy

illustrated by Veronica Terrill

Cover by Ted Warren

Copyright © Good Apple, 1993

ISBN No. 0-86653-743-0

Printing No. 98

Good Apple
A Division of Frank Schaffer Publications, Inc.
23740 Hawthorne Boulevard
Torrance, CA 90505-5927

Table of Contents

GA1458

GA1458

GA1458

Introduction

I Can Write All Through the Year is designed to meet the needs of young children as they develop their first writing skills. The activities follow the themes, seasons, and holidays for a school year. Math, science, and language extension activities are also included. The writing ideas provide a whole language enrichment experience for children in kindergarten, first, or second grade.

The idea for this book originated from the interest in writing exhibited by my kindergarten students at the Independent School. Kindergartners come to school saying, "I can write! See what I wrote!" Unfortunately, teachers often discourage writing until children are able to do it perfectly.

Compare this to spoken language. We are delighted to hear a child's first gurgles. Children are highly praised when their first words are uttered. If a toddler says "mammau" (for *grandma*), we do not correct the child and ask him or her to wait to speak the word until it is pronounced correctly. As a child's speech progresses, he or she gradually gains the ability to enunciate new sounds and build sentence structure.

Reading and writing are also developmental skills. Just as children are immersed in spoken language, they should be given countless opportunities to be immersed in written words.

When a teacher points to a written word as it is spoken, a child can see the relationship between the spoken and written words. Also, a child will begin to see the pattern of reading and writing that moves from the top of the page to the bottom and from the left side of the page to the right side.

Children may participate in reading written words throughout the day. Provide opportunities for shared reading of big books and charts of rhymes, poems, and songs. Reading experience stories, daily stories, innovations of books, graphs, and labels will increase visual stimulation.

Writing at school begins with the teacher modeling or demonstrating all types of writing. When you are setting up the classroom in the fall, ask children to help you write the labels for supplies. For example, when labeling the pencil containers you might have this conversation.

Teacher: What letter sound do you hear at the beginning of *pencils*?

Children: *p* (Teacher writes "p" on the label.)

Teacher: What sound do you hear at the end of *pencils*?

Children: *z* (Teacher explains that the *s* at the end of *pencils* makes a *z* sound and simply writes *s* at the end of the label.)

Teacher: Do you hear any other sounds in *pencils*?

Children: *n* and *l* (Teacher writes *n* and *l* on the label.)

Teacher: There is also an *e*, *c*, and *i* in *pencils*. (Teacher writes these letters in place.)

Children may spell and repeat the word.

Other opportunities to model writing include notes to the principal or parents, field trip notes, observations of science experiments, graphs, labels, captions, time lines, and posters. The overhead projector works nicely for modeling lessons.

At the end of the day, gather the children together and write a daily story. Ask the children "What did you enjoy doing today?" Have the children help you spell the words as you write them on the experience chart. You may include the children's names with their shared comments. At the end of the week these comments may be compiled into a newsletter that is sent home to the family. The children will always look for their names and can usually read their shared comments.

Jill: I played with the hamster.

Matt: We wrote stories on the computer.

Rosa: We made butter by shaking cream.

GA1458

When writing the daily story together, ask questions like those shown below.

"Where on the page do I begin my sentence?"

"What kind of letter do I use for the first word?"

"What do I put at the end of the sentence?"

Children will gradually become more knowledgeable about punctuation, capitalization, spellings of high-frequency sight words, blends, digraphs, vowels, and so on.

During the first writing attempts, encourage the children to listen for sounds they recognize. Encourage a child to "guess" or use invented spelling when a word is not known. Children who know the most frequently used consonant sound can begin to write. Their first attempts at writing are usually simple sentences written to accompany illustrations. Usually only initial sounds of the word are printed.

W R H V C L
We are having a carnival.

As children continue to practice their writing, you will begin to see additional letters in words, correct spacing, and correct sight words. Use of vowels, capitalization, and punctuation will follow.

Notice the [GUESS symbol] symbol on pages where children have guessed or used invented spelling. Children are generally not asked to correct these spellings. If you decide to make a class book for the reading area from the combined pages of the children's work, you use the pages for creating a big book or if the children ask to have their work displayed in the classroom, you may want to edit and recopy the printing. It is important for children to read published material with correct spelling, capitalization and punctuation.

For young children, the teacher or an aide may type or rewrite the children's work. First and second graders may refer to a dictionary for help or ask each other for help in editing their work. The teacher or aide may have conferences with them and then the children may rewrite or use computers to publish their work.

It is helpful to parents if a letter is sent home at the beginning of the year explaining the importance of children's first attempts in writing. You may want to explain the use of invented spelling. A sample letter follows.

Dear Parents,

This year your child will be encouraged to participate in many writing experiences. Research has shown that, with practice, students grow developmentally in writing skills in the same way that children develop spoken language skills by hearing and using a spoken language.

The initial efforts in writing may represent only a single letter of a word (for example, "m" for *mommy*). Gradually your child will progress to several letters per word and will eventually add vowels and correct grammar.

The ☺ symbol indicates that your child is using "guess" or invented spelling. Praise these efforts as you encourage your child to move forward by integrating new learning every day.

If children's work is displayed in the classroom or published for use in the reading area, the children will be editing the spelling and grammar. These papers will then be rewritten. This published work will serve as a model for learning.

Your support is essential to the success and developmental growth of your child's writing skills. If you have any questions regarding this process, please call me. I will welcome your interest.

Sincerely,

How to Use This Book

I Can Write All Through the Year is designed to compliment your whole language program. It does not take the place of handwriting exercises or a writing process program.

You will notice many opportunities for students to illustrate their work. Illustrating helps children define their thoughts and personalize their work. It is an important expression of a child's "own" experience.

The introductory "About Me" section allows children to introduce themselves to the class. "I Am a Super Kid!" reveals something special the child can do. In the "My Feelings" activity, students relate what makes them happy, sad, angry, and scared.

The section "At School" helps children become familiar with classmates, school rules, supplies, and school helpers. "My Special Friends at School" produces a songbook with the names and illustrations of the teacher, principal, secretary, custodian, and a good friend.

On the first day
at Lincoln School
I had a chance to
meet my teacher,
Mr. Lewis.

The book follows the progression of seasons and holidays. A fall activity asks children to sort and graph apples that they bring to class. They may be asked to brainstorm about "Foods Made from Apples." The winter "Experiment with Melting" allows students to predict how long it will take them to melt an ice cube in a plastic bag.

A spring activity challenges students to write a garden vegetable riddle. The "My Lunch" summer activity provides an opportunity for students to plan a lunch using the four basic food groups.

"Halloween Counting Beans" provides an opportunity for students to write numbers in an addition equation. At Thanksgiving children are asked to complete an ABC pattern on an Indian vest.

□ △ ○ □ △ ○ □ △ ○
A B C A B C A B C

"Celebrating Hanukkah" challenges the songwriter to write verses describing ways to celebrate Hanukkah. In the valentine "Friendship Bouquet" the children write about the qualities of a good friend. On the 4th of July, children may design their own flags.

GA1458

Math, science, and language extensions are also included in *I Can Write All Through the Year*. Children record a button sorting activity, spend $100 through catalog shopping, and measure centimeters. Science activities provide for experimentation with magnets, float and sink, and color mixing. Some of the language extensions include innovations on texts and songs, story tape sequencing, and tongue twisters.

Children may work individually or with a partner on most exercises. Many activities lend themselves to cooperative group work. For example, the students are asked to work in small groups to discuss how animals prepare for winter.

The teacher may choose to use an idea as a total class project. For example, the "Friendship Fruit Salad" would work well on a floor graph with the class gathered around.

Writing and reading go hand-in-hand. A child's ability to read is enhanced by practice in writing. As a child increases in reading activity, writing skills will improve proportionately. Writing is a personal experience which requires the child to become totally involved. The student is the doer and not a passive listener.

Children should be provided with writing opportunities every day. By using "guess" or "invented" spelling, children ages 5-7 can express themselves successfully in written language.

 # I Am a Super Kid!

Think of something special you can do. Draw a picture.
Tell what you are doing.

I am a super kid. I can _____

_____

_____

GA1458

All About Me

My name is _____.

I weigh _____ pounds.

I am _____ feet, _____ inches tall.

My hair is _____. (color)

My eyes are _____. (color)

My telephone number is _____.

My address is

_____
(street)

_____
(city)   (state)

_____
(ZIP code)

2

My Birthday

I am _____ years old.

My birthday is on _____ _____.
                                (month)   (day)

Draw the correct number of candles on your cake.

3

GA1458

My Family

Draw a picture of your family.

Tell about something special you like to do with your family.

_____

_____

4

My Feelings

Complete the sentence.
Draw your face.

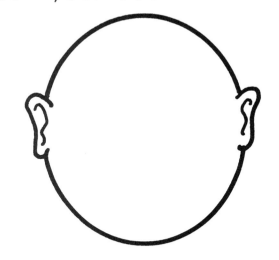

I am happy when _____

_____

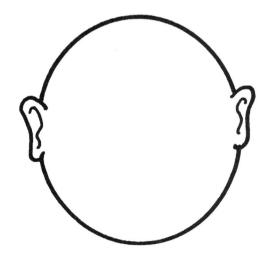

I am sad when _____

_____

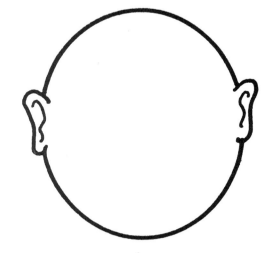

I am angry when _____

_____

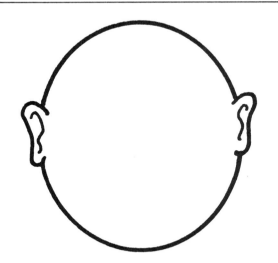

I am scared when _____

_____

GA1458

 # My Hands

Trace your hands.

What can you do with your hands?

My hands can _____

_____

_____

_____

GA1458

My Feet

Trace your feet.

Think about the places you like to go.

My feet like to go _____

_____

_____

_____

My Senses

Our senses help us to learn about the world around us. Our five senses include sight, hearing, smell, taste, and touch. In each circle below write several things that you can see, hear, smell, taste, or touch.

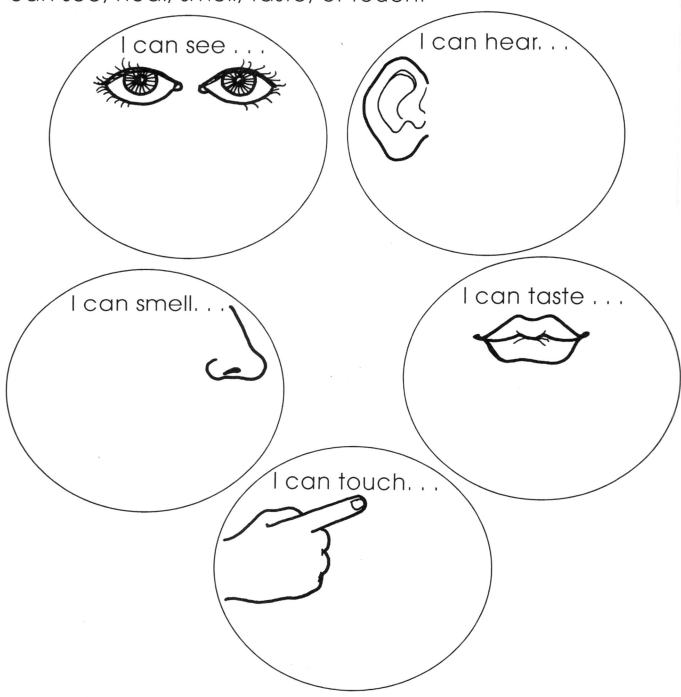

I can see . . .

I can hear. . .

I can smell. . .

I can taste . . .

I can touch. . .

GA1458

My House

This is a picture of my house.

My house has _____ rooms.

My house has _____ doors.

My house has _____ windows.

My house has _____ stairs.

GA1458

When I Grow Up

What will you look like when you are a grown-up? Draw a picture of yourself. Tell what you want to be.

I want to be _____

_____

_____

GA1458

My School

Here is a picture of my school.

_____ School
(name)

The thing I like most about my school is _____

_____

_____

GA1458

Children may make a book of "My Special Friends at School." Each day of the first week of school invite a different helper to visit the classroom. Children may record the visit by writing the visitor's name in their book. (Visitor's name may be posted on chalkboard for reference.) Children may draw or color something that reminds them of that special person.

Cut the pages, arrange in order, and staple into a book.

The verses of each page may be sung to the tune of "The Twelve Days of Christmas."

My Special Friends at School

On the first day at
_____ School
I had a chance to
meet my teacher,
_____.

GA1458

On the second day at
_____ School
I had a chance to
meet the principal,

_____.

On the third day at
_____ School
I had a chance to
meet the secretary,

_____.

On the fourth day at
_____ School
I had a chance to
meet the custodian,

_____.

On the fifth day at
_____ School
I had a chance to
meet a good friend,

_____.

GA1458

My School Supplies

Write the names of your school supplies.

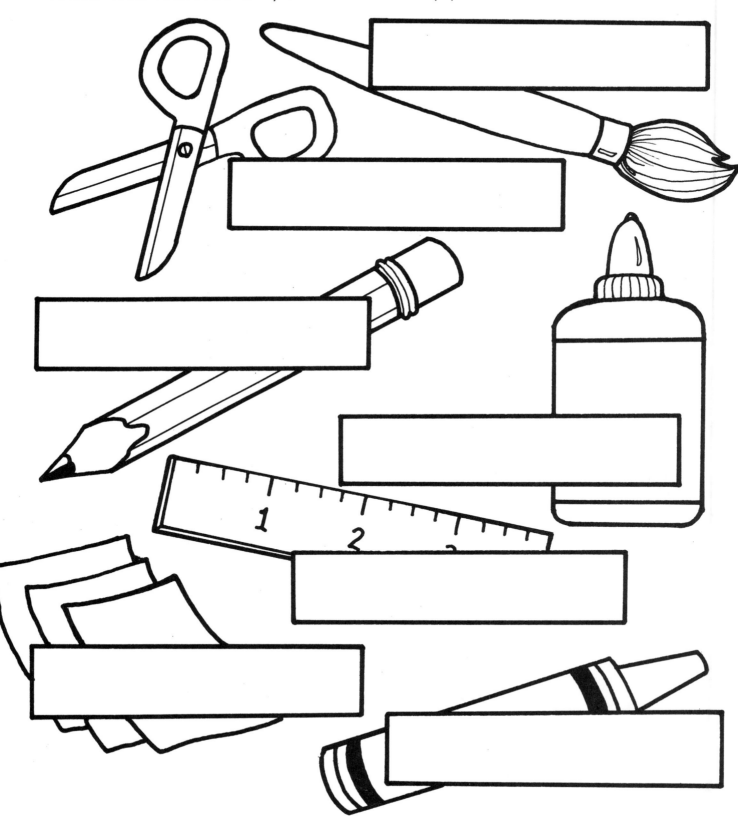

GA1458

My Classmates

Use a class list or desk name tags to copy the names of your classmates.

Girls' Names	Boys' Names

We Are Alike. We Are Different.

Work with a partner. Find ways that you are alike and ways that you are different. Write your answers on the chart below.

We Are Alike	We Are Different

GA1458

Transportation Graph

How do you come to school? Write the names of different kinds of school transportation in the blanks. Color the graph to show how many students use that type of transportation.

Ways We Come to School   **Number of Students**

Ways We Come to School	1	2	3	4	5	6	7	8	9	10	11	12	13	14	15

GA1458

School Rules

Work in small groups. Write a song about your class rules. Use the tune "The Farmer in the Dell" and the pattern aaba. Here is an example.

    We put away our games,
    We put away our games,
    We help our friends. We follow rules.
    We put away our games.

Rule 1

_____

_____

We help our friends. We follow rules.

_____

_____

Rule 2

_____

_____

We help our friends. We follow rules.

_____

My Crayons

Use a matching crayon or marker to trace each color word.

orange

black

red

green

brown

blue

purple

yellow

Color Brainstorming

Work in small groups. Each group chooses a color. Brainstorm within your group. How many things can you think of that are your color? Write your answers on the lines.

Write your color here.

_____

_____   _____

_____   _____

_____   _____

_____   _____

_____   _____

_____   _____

_____   _____

_____   _____

GA1458

Friendship Fruit Salad

If everyone in the class brings a piece of fruit to school, you can make a friendship fruit salad. Sort the fruit. Use the graph to count the fruit. What observations can you make? Enjoy cutting, mixing, and eating fruit salad.

Name of Fruit	How Many?									
	1	2	3	4	5	6	7	8	9	10

Birthday Graph

Cake and ice cream, balloons and gum,
Tell me, when will your birthday come?

Make a class birthday graph. Write the names of your classmates in the right spaces according to the months of their birthdays. Begin in the spaces at the bottom of the graph. Which month had the most birthdays? Which month had the least number of birthdays?

January	February	March	April	May	June

| July | August | September | October | November | December |

GA1458

School Poster

Design a poster for your school. Your poster could be a friendly message to help new children feel welcome. Or it could reflect school spirit. You could remind students to respect school property.

Practice the rough draft for your idea below. Then edit it and copy it on cardboard. Add an illustration or border.

We Fit Together

Dear Parents,
Please help your child write a short story to introduce himself or herself to the class. You might include interests, pets, special summer trips, etc. Also include a photo. The children's photos will be glued together to make a puzzle entitled "We Fit Together."

GA1458

 # A School Song

Use the pattern of the song "Wheels on the Bus" to make a new song about your school. Here is an example.

The principal at the school says,

"Come on in, come on in, come on in."

The principal at the school says, "Come on in"

At _____ School.
              (name)

What will the teacher, children, secretary, custodian, bus driver, etc., say? Write additional verses.

The _____ at the school says,

" _____ "

The _____ at the school says,

_____ "

At _____ School.

_____

The _____ at the school says,

" _____ "

The _____ at the school says,

" _____ "

At _____ School.

Seasons

Weather makes the different seasons of the year. Look at each picture below. Write *Fall, Winter, Spring,* or *Summer* under each picture to tell which season is shown.

GA1458

Adopt a Tree

Walk around your school yard. Find a tree that your class could adopt as their special tree to watch all year.

Touch your tree. Smell your tree. Use a string to measure the *circumference* of the tree. What is special about your tree? Draw a picture of your class tree. Write some words that describe your tree.

28

GA1458

What's in the Feely Box?

Needed:

    Objects in a feely box. (For example, if you are studying trees, you could include a leaf, twig, branch, seed pod, bark, pinecone, root cluster, etc.)

Students may write words to describe one object they touch.

My object felt_____

_____

_____

_____

_____

_____

_____

I think my object was _____

_____

GA1458

Graphing Apples

Needed:
   Have each child bring one
   apple for graphing.

How can you sort the apples?

Color the graph to show how many.

Description of Apples	Number of Apples											
	1	2	3	4	5	6	7	8	9	10	11	12

GA1458

Foods Made from Apples

Many different foods are made from apples. In the apple below write a list of foods that are made from apples.

GA1458

Seeds We Know

Most plants grow from seeds. Each plant has its own kind of seed. We know many of the seeds that we find in fruits and vegetables.

Gather seeds from your neighborhood.

Glue or tape them in the spaces below and label them.

acorn		

GA1458

I Can Explore

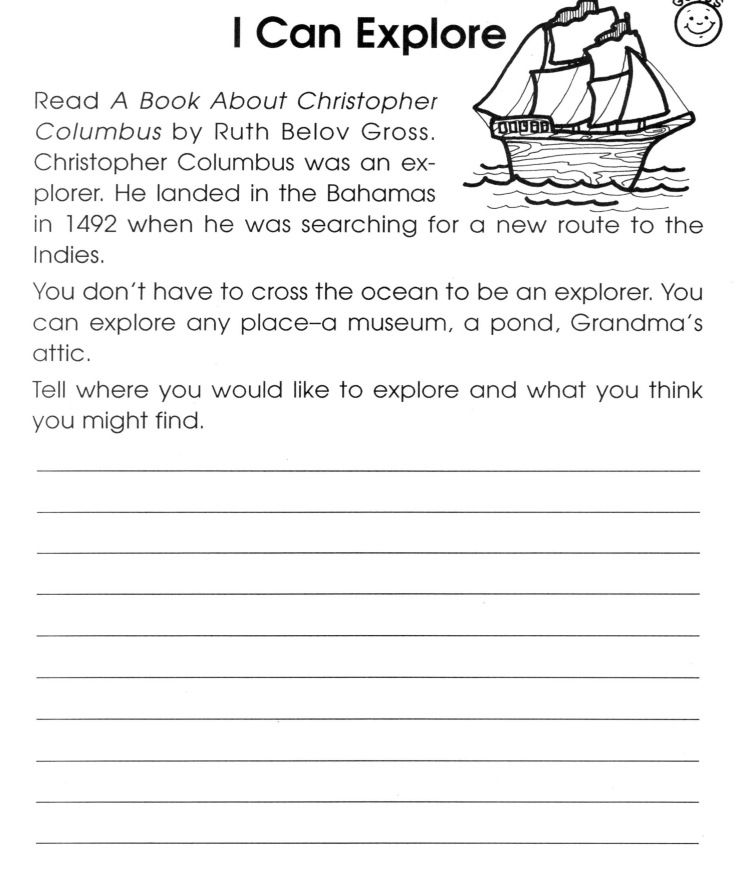

Read *A Book About Christopher Columbus* by Ruth Belov Gross. Christopher Columbus was an explorer. He landed in the Bahamas in 1492 when he was searching for a new route to the Indies.

You don't have to cross the ocean to be an explorer. You can explore any place–a museum, a pond, Grandma's attic.

Tell where you would like to explore and what you think you might find.

_____

_____

_____

_____

_____

_____

_____

_____

_____

GA1458

A Pumpkin Story

The pictures below show the growth of a pumpkin plant. Label each picture. Color and cut pictures out. Put them in order and staple the pages together to make a book that tells the pumpkin story.

34

GA1458

How Many Seeds?

Needed:
 one pumpkin for each small group of students

An adult may help with cutting an opening in the top of a pumpkin. Remove the pulp and seeds. Wash and dry the seeds.

Record the names of friends in your group and their estimates of the number of seeds in the pumpkin. Work together to count the seeds and record the answer.

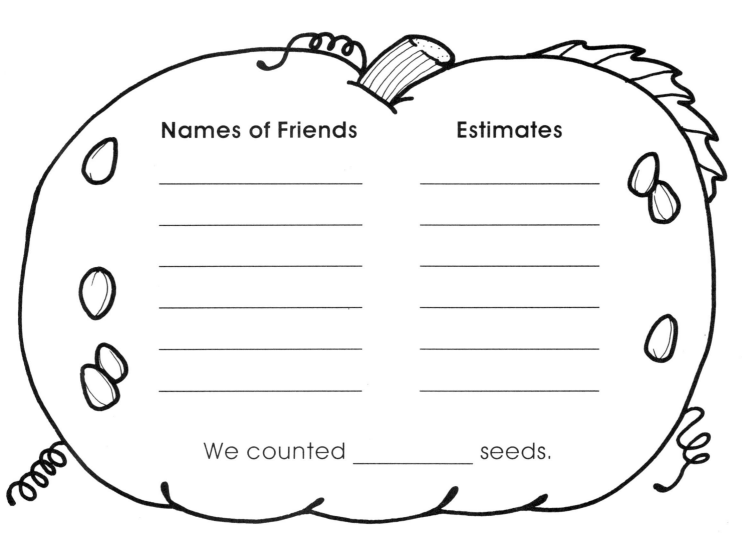

Names of Friends   **Estimates**

_____   _____

_____   _____

_____   _____

_____   _____

_____   _____

_____   _____

We counted _____ seeds.

GA1458

An AB Halloween Pattern

Finish this ab pattern. Draw the picture. Write the word.

witch	ghost				

cat	bat				

36

A Halloween Riddle

Think of a Halloween symbol. Write a riddle about it on the lines at the bottom of this page. On the back of the paper, write the answer to your riddle and draw a picture of it. Here is an example.

front

It is scary.
It is made of bones.
What is it?

back

A skeleton.

_____

_____

_____

_____

What is it?

GA1458

Can You Guess What I Am?

Draw a picture of yourself in your Halloween costume.

I am _____

(name of character)

Halloween Safety

GUESS

What safety tips should you remember when you trick-or-treat on Halloween night?

_____

_____

_____

_____

_____

_____

_____

_____

_____

_____

_____

_____

_____

_____

_____

GA1458

A Scary Adventure

We enjoy lots of scary fun at Halloween. Think about a time when you were really scared. Write about the situation. Tell what happened.

_____

_____

_____

_____

_____

_____

_____

_____

_____

_____

_____

_____

_____

40

GA1458

Halloween Counting Beans

Needed:
   lima bean seeds
   orange spray paint
   black permanent marker

Lay beans on newspaper and paint one side with orange spray paint. Let dry. Use black permanent marker to make ghost eyes on the white side and jack-o'-lantern faces on the orange side. Use these beans for this game.

Place any number of beans in a cup. Shake and pour. Write an addition story.

Example:

$$2 + 3 = 5$$

GA1458

Directions:
Write the word for the picture symbol in the box. Cut out the pages and arrange them in order. Staple the pages.

My Book of Indian Symbols

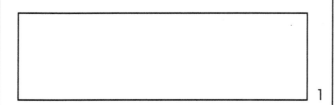

1

2

GA1458

GA1458

Indian Bead Pattern

Write the color words for the ABC Indian bead pattern.
Color the beads.

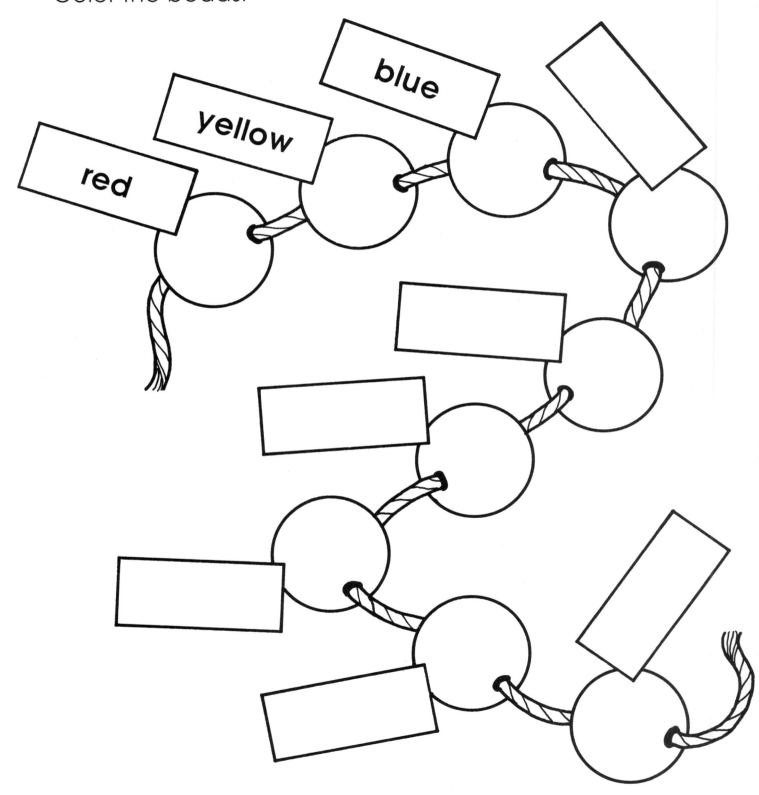

Indian Vest Pattern

Complete the ABC shape pattern on the Indian vest below.

45

GA1458

The Pilgrim Story

Use the tune "Farmer in the Dell" to tell the story of the Pilgrims.

1. They sailed on the *Mayflower*.
   They sailed on the *Mayflower*.
   Many, many years ago,
   They sailed on the *Mayflower*.

2. They landed on Plymouth Rock.
   They landed on Plymouth Rock.
   Many, many years ago,
   They landed on Plymouth Rock.

3. _____

   _____

   Many, many years ago,

   _____

4. _____

   _____

   Many, many years ago,

   _____

Additional verses may be added.

Thanksgiving Day Foods

Read *The Pilgrims' First Thanksgiving* by Ann McGovern. What foods did the Pilgrims and Indians eat at the first Thanksgiving celebration? What foods do you eat at your Thanksgiving dinner? Fill in the chart below.

Foods the Pilgrims and Indians Ate	Foods I Eat

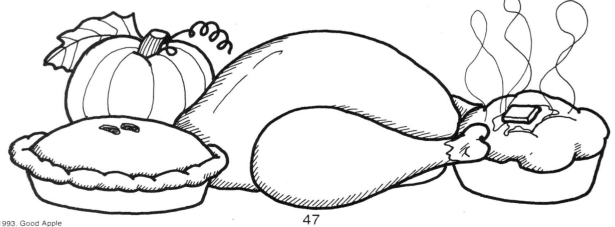

Turkey Talk

What words describe a turkey?
What sounds does he make?
How does he move?
Where is he on Thanksgiving Day?
Using your ideas, write a poem about a turkey.

48

I Am Thankful

Many Pilgrims died during their first winter in America. But by summer, more log cabins had been built. The Pilgrims had made friends with the Indians. Their gardens were rich with food, and they had plenty to eat. The Pilgrims wanted to invite the Indians to a feast and celebrate. They had so much to be thankful for. This was the first Thanksgiving. Tell about things you appreciate.

I am thankful for _____

_____

_____

_____

_____

_____

_____

_____

_____

GA1458

Popcorn for Sale

The Indians taught the Pilgrims how to plant popcorn. Today popcorn is one of our favorite snacks. Work with a partner. List the names of places you can buy popcorn.

Places to Buy Popcorn

_____

_____

_____

_____

_____

_____

_____

_____

_____

GA1458

Animals Prepare for Winter

In many parts of our country winter is a cold season. How do the animals prepare for winter? Work with a partner to complete the chart.

Animals	How They Prepare for Winter
Bears	
Birds	
Snakes	
Rabbits	
Frogs	
Squirrels	
Deer	

51

GA1458

My Winter Clothes

Write the names of the winter clothes below.

GA1458

Penguin Patterns

Complete the ab penguin patterns. Write the words.
Draw the pictures.

front	back				

up	down				

on	off				

Hat Day

Needed:

Invite each child to bring a hat to school for sorting, graphing, storytelling, etc.

red   old
soft   big

In the space below draw your hat. Write words that describe your hat on the lines.

My Hat

_____   _____   _____

_____   _____   _____

_____   _____   _____

GA1458

Experiment with Melting

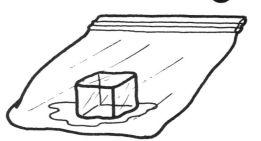

Needed:
   one ice cube in a Zip-
   loc™ bag for each
   child

Work in small groups. Write the names of the students in your group. Predict how many minutes it will take to melt your ice cube. (Do not remove the ice cube from the bag.) Write down your predictions. How long did it actually take to melt your ice cube? Write the outcome.

Names	Prediction	Outcome
	_____ minutes	_____ minutes
	_____ minutes	_____ minutes
	_____ minutes	_____ minutes
	_____ minutes	_____ minutes
	_____ minutes	_____ minutes

GA1458

Celebrating Hanukkah

Use the tune "London Bridge" to create a Hanukkah song. Complete the verses. Here is an example.

We will celebrate Hanukkah, Hanukkah, Hanukkah.
We will celebrate Hanukkah,
By **playing dreidel**.

We will celebrate Hanukkah, Hanukkah, Hanukkah.
We will celebrate Hanukkah,
By _____

We will celebrate Hanukkah, Hanukkah, Hanukkah.
We will celebrate Hanukkah,
By _____

We will celebrate Hanukkah, Hanukkah, Hanukkah.
We will celebrate Hanukkah,
By _____

We will celebrate Hanukkah, Hanukkah, Hanukkah.
We will celebrate Hanukkah,
By _____

GA1458

Menorah Candles

Jewish people light the eight candles of the menorah during the eight days of Hanukkah. The shamush is the helper candle in the middle. It is lighted first and then used to light the other candles. Write the number word on each candle.

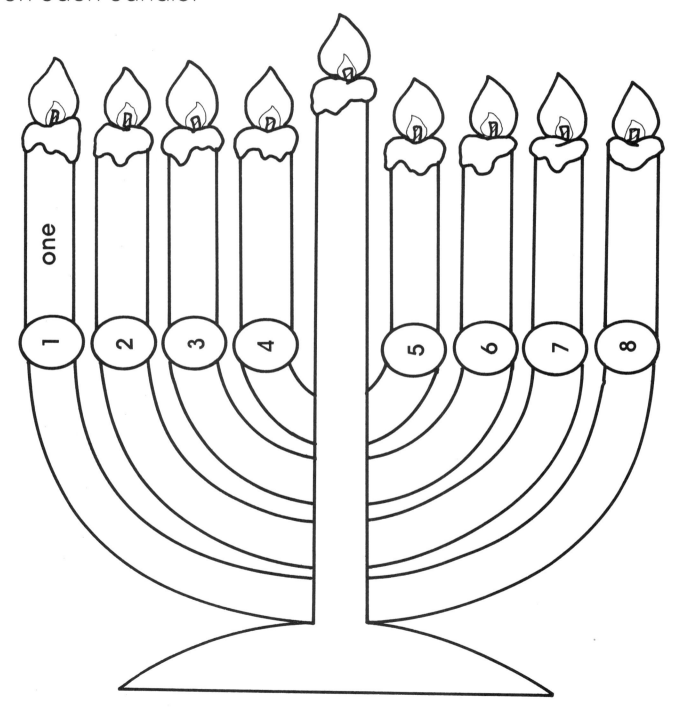

Christmas Web

Make a Christmas web. Children may work individually or in small groups to brainstorm ideas about Christmas. The ideas may be listed in the following categories:

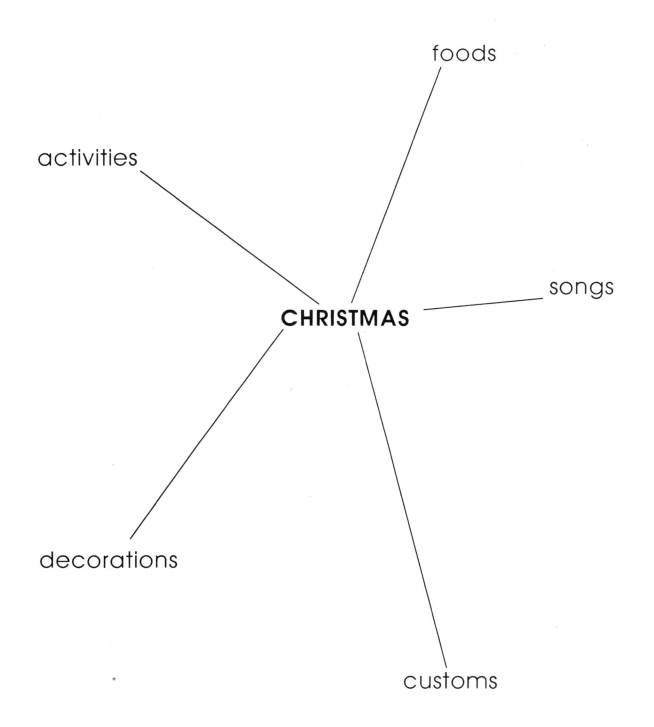

58

Directions:
Label each Christmas light red, orange, yellow, blue, green, or purple. Copy the color word from a classroom color chart. Color the Christmas lights. Cut out the pages and staple them into a book.

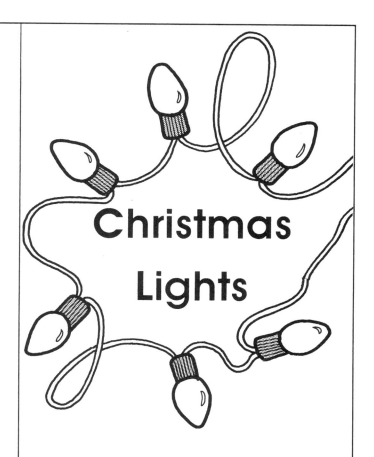

Christmas Lights

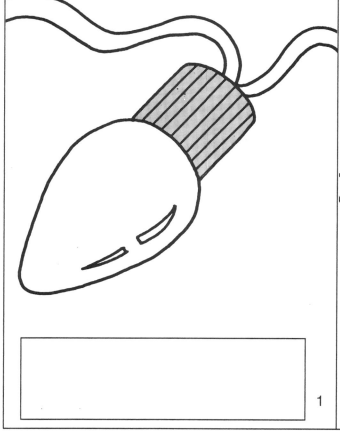

1

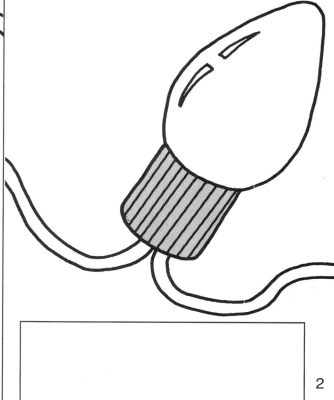

2

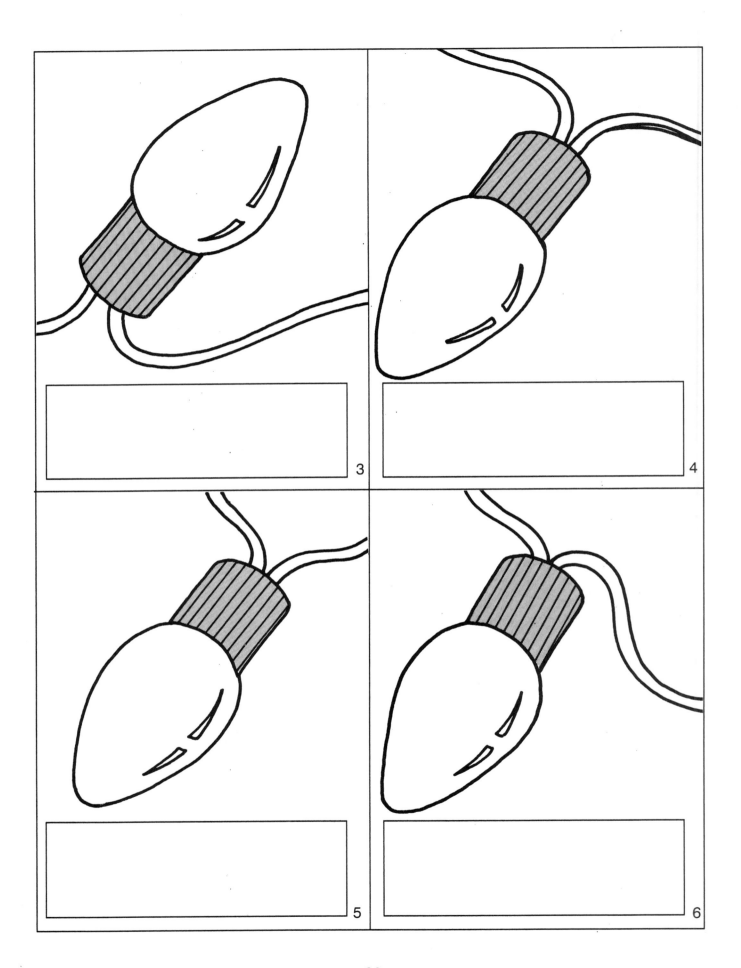

GA1458

Dear Santa,

I can't wait until Christmas.
Cookies and milk will be waiting
for you. Here is my wish list.

_____

_____

_____

_____

_____

_____

Thank you, Santa.

From _____

Thank You

January is an ideal time to write thank-you notes. You may thank friends and relatives for Hanukkah and Christmas presents.

To_____

I say thank you for _____

_____

_____

_____

From _____

To_____

I say thank you for _____

_____

_____

_____

From _____

New Year's Resolution

With the beginning of a new year, people like to think about some changes they can make to improve themselves. These are called "New Year's resolutions." For example, you might say "This year I will make my bed every morning."

Record your New Year's resolution below and illustrate it.

My New Year's resolution is _____

_____

_____

GA1458

The Calendar

Needed:

Ask students to bring old calendars.

Explore the pictures. Recite the months. Count the days in a month. Choose one picture to glue below. Write words that describe your picture.

What words describe this picture?

_____   _____

_____   _____

_____   _____

I Am Changing

Glue your baby picture in the space on the right. Think about ways you have changed since you were a baby. Record your ideas.

_____

_____

_____

_____

_____

_____

_____

_____

_____

_____

_____

GA1458

Groundhog Day

Pretend you are a weather forecaster on Groundhog Day. You are watching a groundhog come out of his burrow. What happens next? What predictions can you make?

DAILY TIMES

February 2

_____

_____

_____

_____

_____

_____

_____

_____

_____

_____

_____

_____

_____

_____

GA1458

Valentine Candy Graphing

Needed:
  small bag of candy conversation hearts for each child

Sort the candy hearts by color. Write the color words in the left column. Color the number spaces to show how many candy hearts you have.

Color	Number								
	1	2	3	4	5	6	7	8	9

GA1458

Friendship Bouquet

What are the qualities of a good friend? Fill the bouquet with friendship thoughts.

68

GA1458

Delicious Valentines

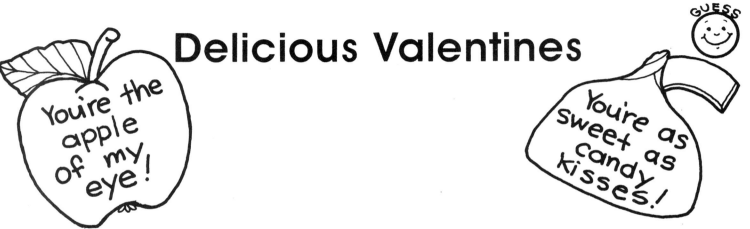

You're the apple of my eye!

You're as sweet as candy kisses!

GUESS

Write a valentine food message. Color it, cut it out and glue it on a red paper heart. Send it to a friend.

69

GA1458

Valentine Song

Use the tune "Skip to My Lou" (pattern aaab) to write a singing valentine. Here are two examples.

Candy, red and white,
Candy, red and white,
Candy, red and white,
Share it with a friend.

Make a valentine,
Make a valentine,
Make a valentine,
Share it with a friend.

Valentine Song

_____

_____

_____

_____

_____

_____

 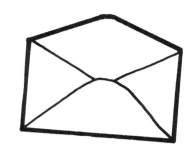

Valentine Envelopes

Send a valentine to a friend or relative. Practice writing your friend's address below. Then copy the address on the valentine envelope.

_____
(name)

_____
(street)

_____ , _____ _____
(city)   (state)   (ZIP code)

GA1458

Martin Luther King, Jr.

Martin Luther King, Jr., was upset because African Americans did not have the rights to live, work, or go to school wherever they wished. Rev. King worked hard in a non-violent way to change unfair laws. We will remember Martin Luther King, Jr., for his dream of a nation where people are judged by their character and not by the color of their skin. What is your dream or wish for the future?

GA1458

Black History

February is Black History Month. Choose an African American leader. (Some suggestions follow.) Use reference books to find the information below.

Harriet Tubman	Frederick Douglass
Martin Luther King, Jr.	Garrett A. Morgan
Wilma Rudolph	Thurgood Marshall
Shirley Chisolm	Duke Ellington
Jackie Robinson	Guion S. Bluford, Jr.
Rosa Parks	George Washington Carver

Name: _____

Birthplace: _____

Childhood Events: _____

_____

_____

_____

Why is this person remembered? _____

_____

_____

_____

_____

GA1458

Famous Americans

Presidents' Day is a holiday that honors two famous American Presidents, Abraham Lincoln and George Washington. We have cities, monuments, buildings, streets, and other things named for Abraham Lincoln and George Washington.

Work in small groups. Think of places you know that have been named after famous Americans.

Famous Americans	Places Named for Famous Americans
John F. Kennedy	Kennedy Space Center

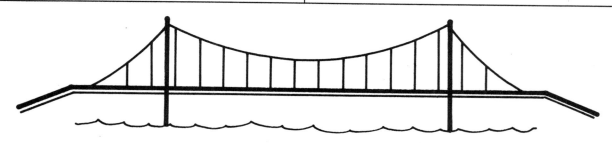

GA1458

George Washington Words

How many words can you make from the letters in *George Washington?*

Example: shine

_____

_____

_____

_____

_____

_____

_____

_____

_____

_____

GA1458

Good Luck, Bad Luck

Finding a four-leaf clover is supposed to bring you good luck. What good luck have you had? What bad luck have you had?

GA1458

Spring Poem

Write a poem about spring using these four parts.

1. a color
2. an object
3. an action
4. Spring is here!

Example: Yellow
Daffodils
Standing tall
Spring is here!

Spring Poem

(color)_____

(object)_____

(action)_____

Spring is here!

GA1458

Spring Rebus Story

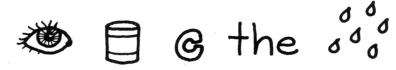

👁 🗄 @ the 💧💧💧

The 🐥🐥 R eating 〰〰

What are the signs of spring in your neighborhood? Use rebus symbols where possible to write your spring story.

Spring Story

Use the pattern in *Brown Bear, Brown Bear, What Do You See?* by Bill Martin, Jr., to write a spring story. Work in groups of eight to ten. Think of signs of spring. Complete the pattern. Illustrate the pages. Bind them into a book and make a cover.

"Earthworm, Earthworm, What do you see?"

"I see a robin looking at me."

_____

_____

What do you see?

I see _____

looking at me!

GA1458

We Hatch from Eggs

Read *Chickens Aren't the Only Ones* by Ruth Heller. Think of different birds and animals that could hatch from this egg. Write your ideas inside the egg.

Bunny Banter

If possible, bring a pet bunny into the classroom. Students may work with partners to brainstorm about bunnies. Compete the web.

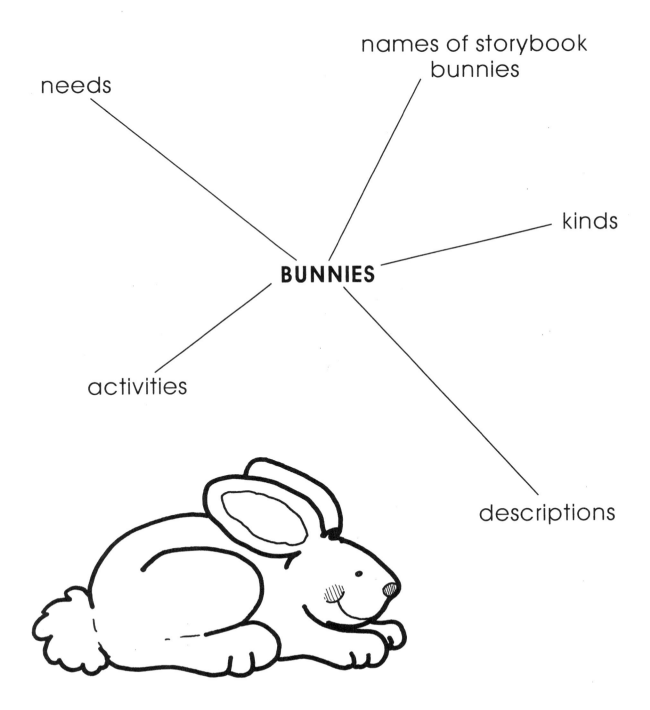

needs

names of storybook bunnies

kinds

BUNNIES

descriptions

activities

Funny Bunny

What can this funny bunny do? Use magazines and catalogs to find something interesting to add to this bunny. Cut out and glue your addition. Complete the funny bunny story.

This funny bunny wears sunglasses.

_____
_____
_____
_____
_____
_____
_____
_____
_____
_____
_____

Jelly Bean Graphing

Copy the color words from the classroom color chart.
Graph ten jelly beans. Count and compare.

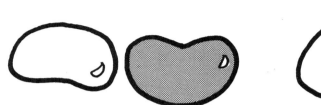

Color Words

	1	2	3	4	5

GA1458

We Need Trees

Trees are the earth's only renewable resource. That means, if a tree is cut for lumber, a new tree can be planted to replace it. What are some of the uses of trees? Write your ideas below.

Uses for Trees

_____

_____

_____

_____

_____

_____

_____

_____

_____

_____

_____

_____

GA1458

The Parts of a Tree

Label the parts of the tree.
 roots
 trunk
 branch
 leaf
 blossom

GA1458

Keeping the Earth Clean

When air, land, or water becomes dirty, we say it is polluted. We know that polluted air, land, and water are harmful to plants, animals, and people. We are the caretakers of the earth. How can we keep our earth clean? Work with a partner. Write your ideas below.

_____

_____

_____

_____

_____

_____

_____

_____

_____

_____

_____

_____

_____

GA1458

The Parts of a Plant

Label the parts of the plant.
roots
stem
leaf
blossom

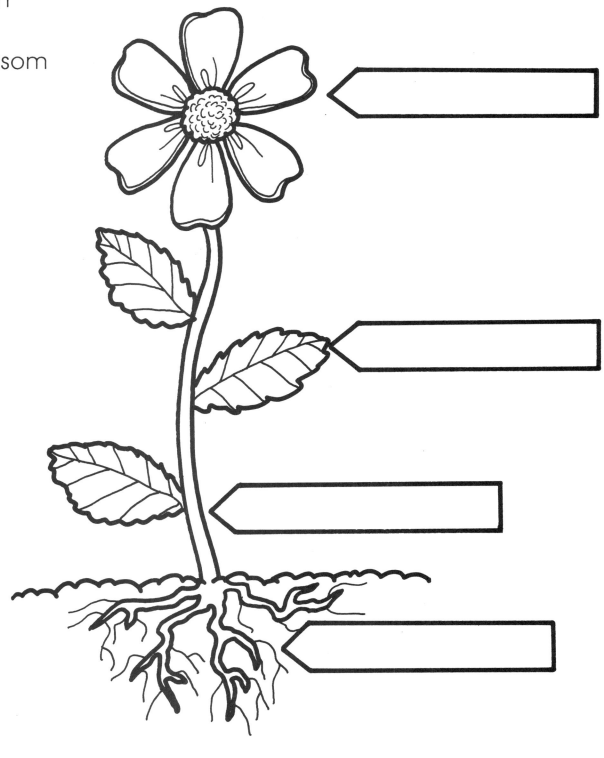

GA1458

Vegetables We Eat

We can eat different parts of a plant. Think about vegetables in a garden. What part do you eat–the root, the stem and the leaves, or the seeds? List several vegetables under each heading.

What Do You Eat?

Roots	Stems and Leaves	Seeds

GA1458

Vegetable Garden Riddle

Think of a vegetable that grows in a garden.

Write a riddle on a 6" x 6" flip-up sheet of paper and glue below.

Illustrate your vegetable riddle and write the answer in the space below.

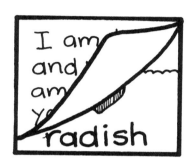

---------------------------------- Glue riddle here. ----------------------------------

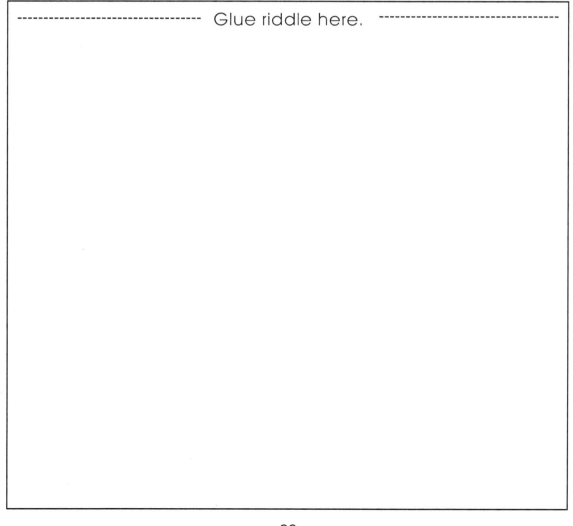

GA1458

Weighing a Pound

Needed:

    Invite each child to bring one vegetable to be used for sorting and weighing.

    a scale

Sort the vegetables. Weigh each group to see how many equal a pound. (If there are not enough, make an estimate.)

How Many?	Name of Vegetable	1 Pound
		1 pound
		1 pound
		1 pound
		1 pound
		1 pound
		1 pound
		1 pound
		1 pound

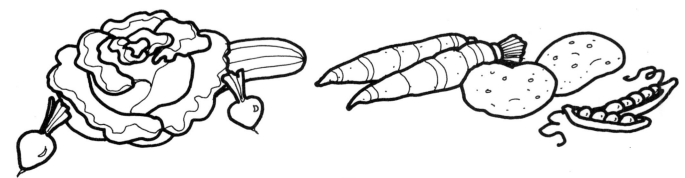

What's in Your Yard?

Brainstorm with the class to list "things found in a yard." Use a tally to record the number of classmates with items in each category.

What's in Your Yard?	Tally

GA1458

Diary of Bug Business

What do insects do all day? Take fifteen minutes of class time every day for one week. Find an insect. Write your observation of what the insect is doing.

	Name of Insect	Observation
Monday		
Tuesday		
Wednesday		
Thursday		
Friday		

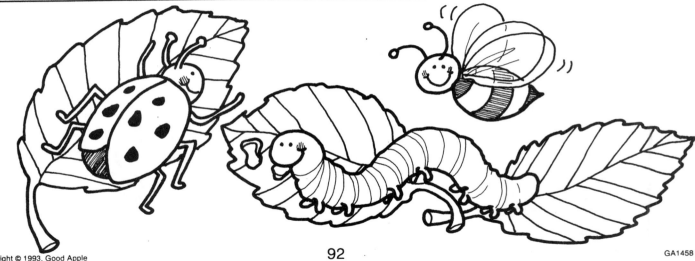

GA1458

Complete the Mother's Day message. Add an illustration.

Dear Mother,

I love you more than _____

_____

_____

_____

GA1458

Make an end-of-school autograph book. Cut and staple pages into a book. Ask friends to sign your autograph book. Additional pages may be added.

_____'s
(name)

Autograph
Book

GA1458

Happy Father's Day

Complete the Father's Day spell-out.

F is for _____

A is for _____

T is for _____

H is for _____

E is for _____

R is for _____

Put them all together they spell FATHER, the one who's special all year long!

GA1458

Summertime

Enjoy the story *Yonder* by Tony Johnston. Notice how the author explores the seasons of life. She ends many pages with the words "There. Just over there." Think about the season of summer. Write sentences to describe summer in your neighborhood. End with the words "There. Just over there."

Illustrate your words.

_____

_____

_____

_____

There. Just over there.

Bicycle Safety Rules

What safety habits should you practice when riding your bicycle? Work with a partner. Write your ideas below.

1. _____

_____

2. _____

_____

3. _____

_____

4. _____

_____

5. _____

_____

6. _____

_____

GA1458

Transportation

Transportation is a way of carrying people and things from one place to another. There are many different types of transportation. Work with a partner. Place your ideas under the headings Land, Air, or Water.

Kinds of Transportation

Land	Air	Water

At the Beach

Experiment: How is ocean water different from fresh water?

Mix salt and water in one dish.
Put fresh water in another dish.

Make a prediction below of what you think will happen.

Observe the dishes in a few days and record the results.

Prediction:
Results:

At the Zoo

Lions that roar and cows that moo,
Tell me your favorite animal at the zoo.

Illustrate your favorite animal.

My favorite animal is _____

because _____

_____

100

Zoo Rhyming Riddle

Choose a zoo animal. Write a riddle.
Include a rhyme. Illustrate your riddle.

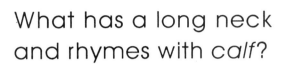

What has a long neck
and rhymes with *calf*?

GA1458

Fourth of July Graph

How do you celebrate the 4th of July? List activities that your family enjoys on the 4th of July. Graph the number of children participating in each activity.

Activity	Number													
	1	2	3	4	5	6	7	8	9	10	11	12	13	14
watch fireworks														
swim														
watch parade														

GA1458

Our Flag

The first American flag had 13 stripes and 13 stars to represent the 13 colonies. Today our flag still has the 13 stripes, but we have 50 stars to represent our 50 states. If you were asked to design a flag for the United States, what would it look like? Draw your design below.

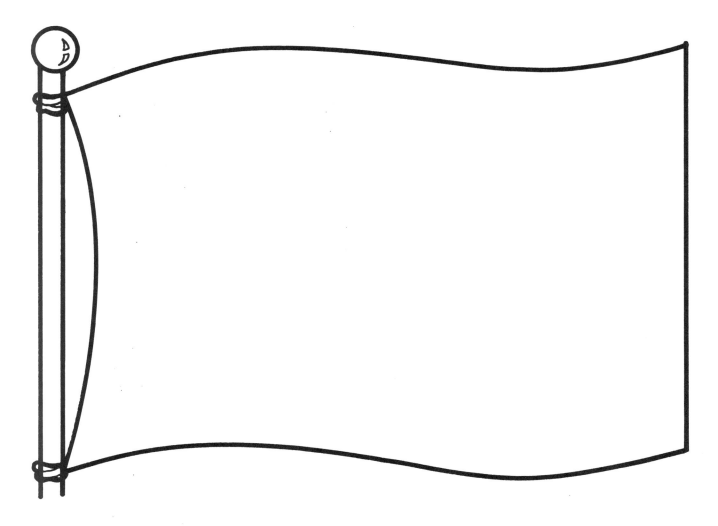

Tell about your design. _____

_____

_____

_____

GA1458

Good for You

Look through magazines. Find snacks that are good for you. Cut out pictures and glue below. Label the pictures.

104

GA1458

Basic Food Groups

The foods we eat can be grouped in the following way:
    fruits and vegetables
    breads and cereals
    milk and milk products
    meat and eggs

Think of examples for each group. Write your ideas below.

meat and eggs

fruits and vegetables

milk and milk products

breads and cereals

GA1458

My Lunch

Plan a lunch. Choose something from each food group. Illustrate on the plate below.

The fruit or vegetable is _____

The bread or cereal is _____

The milk product is _____

The meat (or egg) is _____

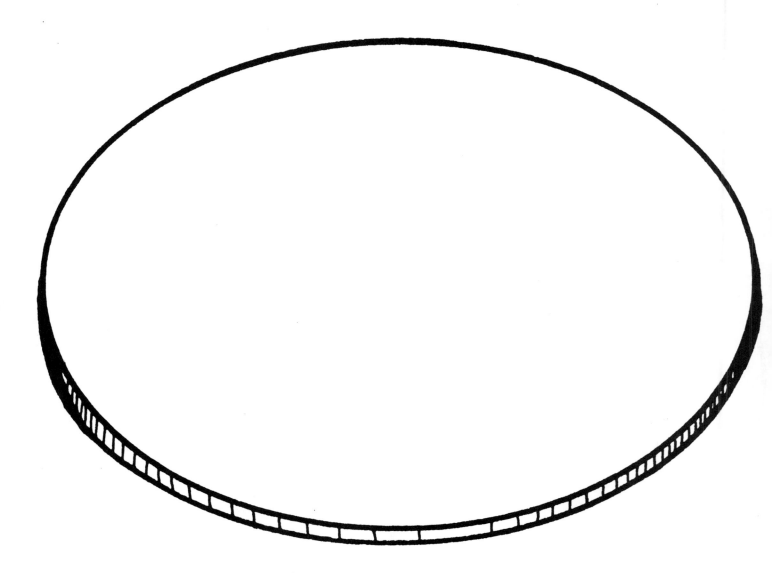

What Is Your Favorite Sandwich?

Write the recipe for your favorite kind of sandwich. Give it a name.

Include any special instructions.

GA1458

Button Sorting

Needed:
   one plastic bag with ten buttons for each pair of students

Work with a partner. Brainstorm different ways to sort the buttons. Record the results.

Example: 2 holes	more than 2 holes

GA1458

Thinking About Shapes

Look around the classroom. Think about objects in your home and environment.

List objects that are shaped like a circle, square, triangle, or rectangle.

Circle ◯ Example: record	**Square** ☐
Triangle △	**Rectangle** ▭

GA1458

My Dozen Design

Needed:
   paper pattern block shapes

Students may use a dozen pattern block shapes to make a design. Glue the design. Describe your design.

My design looks like _____

_____

Where Is the Triangle?

Find the correct word. Fill in the space.

over or under _____	on or off _____
right or left _____	top or bottom _____
in or out _____	high or low _____
above or below _____	in front of or behind _____

GA1458

Sorting Coins

Needed:
    a handful of coins for each student

Students may sort the coins. Color to graph.

Value	Name of Coin	Number of Coins								
		1	2	3	4	5	6	7	8	9
1¢										
5¢										
10¢										
25¢										
50¢										

GA1458

Spending $100

You have $100 to spend. Look at a catalog. What will you buy? List the things you would buy and the prices below. Do not spend more than $100. How much money is remaining?

Items Bought	Price
Total	

Roll and Count

Needed:
  one die for each student

Roll the die. Draw the dots. Write the number word.

Example:	
two	_____
_____	_____
_____	_____
_____	_____

GA1458

Twos and Threes

Work in small groups to think of things that come in 2s and 3s. Record your ideas. (Magazines, catalogs, and newspapers may be helpful for ideas.)

Things That Come in 2s	Things That Come in 3s

GA1458

Book of 6s

Needed:
   a variety of objects for gluing (old stamps, toothpicks, buttons, stickers, wallpaper pieces, pattern block shapes)

Glue six objects on each page. Let them dry. Label the objects. Cut out the pages and staple them into a "Book of Six."

Book
of
Six

6 _____

6 _____

6 _____

Measuring Inches

Needed:
  rulers and yardsticks

Students may measure objects in the classroom. Write down each object measured and the length of the object. Illustrate the object.

I measured _____.

It was _____ inches.

I measured _____.

It was _____ inches.

I measured _____.

It was _____ inches.

I measured _____.

It was _____ inches.

I measured _____.

It was _____ inches.

GA1458

Measuring a Foot

Needed:
   tubs of objects for measuring (Example: unifix cubes,
      beans, paper clips, pattern blocks, pom-poms, etc.)
   rulers

Place the like objects in a straight line to equal one foot.
Record your work.

Object	How Many = 1 Foot?
Example: pennies	16

GA1458

Measuring Centimeters

Needed:
   a ruler which measures centimeters for each child

Estimate how many centimeters each object is. Then measure and record.

	Estimate	Measure
My shoe		
My hand		
My favorite book		
A pencil		
A crayon		
A key		
Scissors		

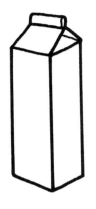

GUESS

Cup, Pint, Quart, and Gallon

Things You Can Purchase by the Cup	Things You Can Purchase by the Pint
Things You Can Purchase by the Quart	**Things You Can Purchase by the Gallon**

GA1458

Liter

less than
1 liter

1 liter

more than
1 liter

How much liquid does each hold? Is it more or less than 1
liter? Write *more* or *less*.

_____

_____

_____

_____

_____

_____

How Long Is a Minute?

Think of an activity you can do. How many times can you do it in one minute? What is your prediction? Now time yourself. What was your result?

In One Minute I Can . . .	Prediction	Result
jump rope		
write the numbers from 1 to ___		
hop on 2 feet		
name _____ animals		
make a paper clip chain with _____ paper clips		

GA1458

My Daily Schedule

What is your daily schedule? Record the time and activities of your daily routine.

Time	Activity
	Get up
	Eat breakfast
	Go to school

GA1458

sunny   rainy   snowy   cloudy   windy

Weather Chart

Keep a record of the weather. Use the symbol and word *sunny, rainy, snowy, cloudy,* or *windy* to show the weather each day.

	_____ (month)				
	Mon.	Tues.	Wed.	Thurs.	Fri.
First Week					
Second Week					
Third Week					
Fourth Week					

What Does a Magnet Attract?

Collect a group of objects. (Example: nail, pencil, small wooden bead, paper clip, coin, crayon, spoon, plastic toy, key, feather, cork, etc.)

Predict which ones the magnet will attract. Test each object with a magnet. Record your results below.

Attracts	Does Not Attract

GA1458

Float and Sink

Needed:
  a tub of water
  objects for testing (cork, pencil, marble, small bottle,
    paper clip, Styrofoam™ cup, rock, crayon, plastic
    toy, etc.)

Predict which objects will float and which ones will sink.
Test each object in the tub of water. Record your results.

Things That Float	Things That Sink

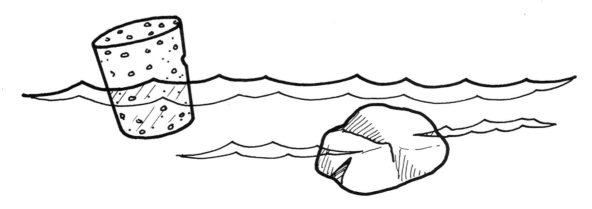

Color Mixing

Needed:
   three juice glasses with water
   red, blue, and yellow food coloring
   medicine droppers
   small bottles for mixing colors
   paper towels

Add several drops of red food coloring to one glass. Do the same with yellow and blue food coloring. Use medicine droppers and small bottles to mix colors.

red + blue = _____

red + yellow = _____

blue + yellow = _____

Color the wheel below to show your results.

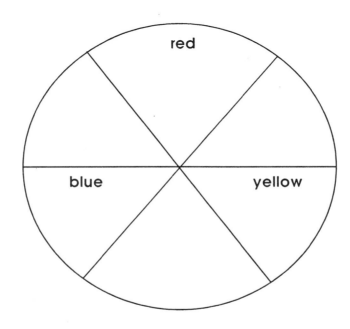

GA1458

Dinosaur Dinners

Using the resources from the library, copy the names of some dinosaurs. Consider their teeth, how they walked, and where they lived. Were they plant eaters or meat eaters? Fill in the chart below.

Dinosaur Dinners

Name of Dinosaur	Plant or Meat Eater?

GA1458

Dinosaur Details

Choose a dinosaur. Using a resource book, find the following details about your dinosaur.

1. Name: _____

2. Size: _____

3. Food Eaten: _____

4. Description: _____

_____

_____

_____

_____

_____

5. Special Characteristics: _____

_____

_____

GA1458

Liquids, Solids, and Gases

Compare a bowl of water, a rock, and a balloon filled with air. Does a liquid have a special shape? Does the rock change shape when it is moved? Can you see a gas? Does the gas occupy a space?

Think of examples of liquids, solids, and gases. Fill in the chart below.

Liquids	Solids	Gases
Example: water	Example: rock	Example: air

GA1458

Gifts from the Sun

The sun is our closest star. It is 93,000,000 miles from the earth. Without the sun there would be no life on our planet. Think of the many gifts we get from the sun. Record them below.

Gifts from the Sun

Living Things

Plants and animals are both living things. Draw a picture of a plant and an animal.

Plant	**Animal**

How are they alike? _____

_____

_____

How are they different? _____

_____

_____

GA1458

Habitat

The place where a plant or animal naturally lives is called its habitat. Brainstorm with a partner. What plants and animals would you find in the habitats below?

Woods

Desert

Ponds

Oceans

Pet Diary

What kind of pets do you have in your classroom or at home? Watch your pet. Tell about something your pet does each day.

On Monday _____ _____
                    (name of pet)   (activity of pet)

_____

On Tuesday _____ _____

_____

On Wednesday _____ _____

_____

On Thursday _____ _____

_____

On Friday _____ _____

_____

GA1458

Bean Experiment

Needed:
    clear plastic cups
    paper towels
    lima beans that have been
      soaked overnight

Place a lima bean on the inside wall of the cup. Wet a paper towel and place around the inside of the cup.

What do you think will happen to the bean? Make a prediction.

Observe the lima bean for five to ten days.
What happened to the bean? Record your results.

Prediction:

Results:

Do Plants Drink Water?

Fill two glasses with water.
Add red food coloring to one glass.
Add blue food coloring to the other.

Place one celery stem in the glass with red water.
Place another celery stem in the glass with blue water.

What do you predict will happen?
Make a prediction.

Observe for several days. Record your results.

Prediction:
Results:

GA1458

Fire Safety

Look at each picture and read what is happening. How should you respond?

What should I do if there is a fire in my house?

_____

_____

_____

What should I do if I get a burn from hot water, a hot iron, or a hot stove?

_____

_____

_____

What should I do if my clothes catch on fire?

_____

_____

What number should I call to report a fire?

_____

GA1458

Buckle Up

When riding in a car, it is important to "buckle up." Wearing a seat belt protects you from being injured.

Design a poster for seat belt safety. Write a rule for wearing seat belts.

Rule: _____

_____

_____

GA1458

Reporting from
Mother Goose Land

You are a news reporter gathering information for a story.
Choose a nursery rhyme. Answer the five questions.

Who?

What?

Where?

When?

How?

139

GA1458

A Story Tape Sequence

Listen to a story tape. Recall the order of events in the story. Tell what happened in the beginning, middle, and ending of the story.

_____
(name of story tape)

Beginning

Middle

Ending

GA1458

Innovations on Text

In *The Very Hungry Caterpillar* by Eric Carle, the sentence "On Monday he ate through one apple" is changed to different days and different foods. How many ways can you change this sentence from *The Three Billy Goats Gruff*?

Once upon a time . . .

Yesterday
Last week
On Friday

Once upon a time	there were three billy goats	who were going up the hill	to make themselves fat.

GA1458

Tongue Twisters

Read Beau Gardner's *Have You Ever Seen . . .?*

Choose a letter of the alphabet and write a tongue twister. Illustrate.

Have you ever seen . . .

two tired tigers on a trip?

Have you ever seen . . .

What Are You Wearing?

Enjoy *Mary Wore Her Red Dress* by Merle Peek. Students may change the verse to reflect what they are wearing. Illustrate the verse. An example follows.

Robert wore his blue jeans,
Blue jeans, blue jeans.
Robert wore his blue jeans,
All day long.

_____

_____

_____

All day long.

GA1458

Winter Words

Read *The Mitten* adapted and illustrated by Jan Brett. Examine the detailed borders. In the frame below design your own winter border. In the middle space write words that describe winter weather, clothes, activities, and sports.

If the Dinosaurs Came Back

Read *If the Dinosaurs Came Back* by Bernard Most. Think of your own idea of how your neighborhood would be different. Draw a picture. Complete the sentence.

If the dinosaurs came back _____

_____

_____

GA1458

Story Map

Read *We're Going on a Bear Hunt* retold by Michael Rosen. Make an illustrated map and captions to tell the sequence of the story. You will need to tape additional pages on the right side (accordion style) to make a long map.

A House Is a House for Me

Read *A House Is a House for Me* by Mary Ann Hoberman. Think of another "_____ is a house for _____" innovation. Write your idea below and illustrate.

The sky is a house for the stars.

_____ is a house for _____ .

GA1458

"Mama Don't Allow"

Enjoy the story/song "Mama Don't Allow" by Thacher Hurd. Think of new verses you could add. Here is an example.

Papa don't allow no bubble gum chewing 'round here.

Write your new verse below and illustrate.

_____

_____

_____

_____

_____

GA1458

Daily Story

What did you do in school today? Record the date. Tell about the activities you did today.

Today is _____, _____ _____, _____
              (day of week)   (month)   (day)   (year)

_____

_____

_____

_____

_____

_____

_____

Field Trip Observation

Date:_____

Place Visited: _____

Observation: _____

_____

_____

_____

_____

_____

_____

_____

_____

Favorite Part of the Trip: _____

_____

_____

_____

_____

GA1458